A GUIDE TO
ZUNI FETISHES
AND CARVINGS

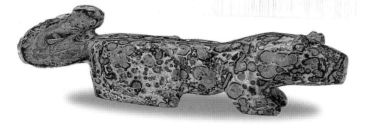

by Kent McManis

Photography by Robin Stancliff

TREASURE CHEST BOOKS
TUCSON, ARIZONA

ACKNOWLEDGMENTS

This book would never have come about had it not been for so many people urging and helping me to write it. First, to my wife Laurie who sparked my interest in fetishes and did so much work on this project, my immeasurable love and gratitude. Everything I have done in my life, I could not have done without her. Thanks to Corilee Sanders, Micheal Dunham, Melissa Casagrande, and Darcy Dishta for their special help. Their extra efforts, input, and generous gifts of time and knowledge have been invaluable. Thanks to Sterling Mahan for patiently pushing me to write this book; to Donald Sharp for his encouragement and information; to Pat Harrington and Joe and Cindy Tanner for historical help; to Joan Caballero, John Kania, and Joe Ferrin for showing me the beauty of old fetishes; and to Darlene and Joe Foster for early support on this project. Picture-perfect thanks to Robin Stancliff for all the exceptional photographs that give "life" to these pages. Thanks to Mark Bahti and Bob Jeffries for putting up with me. A heartfelt "I miss you" and eternal thanks to John Stone, my trader friend, and to Bill Adams, the man who taught me so much. And a very special thanks to all the countless people at Zuni who were so giving with their priceless help and wisdom and for being such incredible craftspeople. *Elahkwa.*

TREASURE CHEST BOOKS
P. O. Box 5250
Tucson, AZ 85703-0250
(520) 623-9558

ISBN 0-918080-77-0   Library of Congress No.95-61012

Title page photo: fetish by Marlo Booqua, leopard stone mountain lion.

All fetishes pictured are courtesy of Grey Dog Trading Co. and private collections.

This book is set in Bitsteam Charter and ITC Goudy Sans.
Edited by Linnea Gentry
Designed by Paul Mirocha
Printed in Korea

CONTENTS

INTRODUCTION

IF YOU SAY THE WORD "FETISH" TO most people, an image of a small carving does not usually come to mind. But "fetish" is the conventional term to describe one of these delightful Native American carvings, even though charm or talisman may be more appropriate. A fetish is an object believed to have a power greater than the object itself would naturally possess. A fetish that has been ceremonially blessed by a priest or shaman would be considered a "true" fetish by most Native Americans. And it could then serve different religious or magical purposes. Most of the fetishes created today might best be called "carvings," because they are made as art objects. But they could become true fetishes if properly blessed and used.

While many Native American tribes produce and use fetishes, the most renowned fetish carvers are undoubtedly the Zuni, or Asiwi (AH-she-wee) as they call themselves. They are one of the largest Pueblo tribes of the Southwest. Like other Pueblo peoples, the Zuni live a farming-oriented lifestyle in relatively permanent villages. While agriculture is not as all-encompassing for contemporary Zuni, it remains an important religious focus. Most Pueblo tribes share a similar cultural heritage, but the Zuni have a unique feature. Their language is not closely related to any other in the region.

The ancestors of the present-day Zuni arrived in the area about 700-800 AD and by the sixteenth century occupied about 500 households in several separate villages. A Spanish expedition led by the Franciscan friar Marcos de Niza made the first European contact with Zuni in 1536 during their search for the Seven Cities of Cíbola. Francisco Vasquez de Coronado and his troops returned in 1540 and defeated the Zuni during their exploration of the greater southwestern area. More Spaniards soon followed. The Pueblo Revolt succeeded in driving them out in 1680, but by 1692 the Spanish were back to stay.

Americans pressing west from the eastern part of the continent began to pass through Zuni in the 1800's. The railroad reached nearby Gallup in 1881,

dramatically opening up the area to outside influences. Two years before, the Bureau of American Ethnology had sent the first anthropological expedition to Zuni, a group which included James and Matilda Coxe Stevenson and Frank H. Cushing. Much of our knowledge about Zuni culture and fetishes of the time comes from their research.

Today, one main village remains on the site of the old village of Halona:wa (HAH-low-nah-WAH), about 35 miles south of Gallup, New Mexico. The Zuni Reservation also includes the housing development of Black Rock and a few small satellite farming communities. The tribe consists of around 9,000 people (large compared to most Pueblo populations) on lands totaling about 400,000 acres.

Like many other Native Americans, Zunis have long carried interesting or unusual "charm stones," believing they bring luck, power, or protection. Stones that naturally look like animals, or even humans or deities, are often called concretion fetishes. Concretions and stones that require very little carving to bring out an image are considered more powerful than fetishes that require a great deal of carving. The reason lies in Zuni mythology.

The Zuni believe that the world was once covered with floodwaters which left it swampy. The Sun Father, revered by the Zuni as the giver of life and light, created twin sons. The Twins realized the world was too wet for humankind to survive and needed to be dried. The Sun Father had given his sons a magic shield, a bow (the rainbow), and arrows (lightning). The Twins placed their shield on the earth, crossed the rainbow and lightning arrows on top of it, and shot an arrow into the point where they crossed. Lightning flew out in every direction, creating a tremendous fire. Although this dried the earth, it made it too easy for predators to catch and eat people. So to save humanity, the Twins struck these animals with their lightning, burning and shrivelling them into stone. But deep within, the animals' hearts were kept alive, with instructions to help humankind with the magic captured in their hearts. When a Zuni finds a stone that naturally resembles an animal, he believes that it is one of these ancient stone beasts.

While most Zuni fetishes today look considerably different from simply formed fetishes of the past, the core beliefs surrounding them remain. This book will help answer questions about fetishes and the people who make them. It is designed to provide a concise and easy-to-use guide for people buying either their first Zuni fetish or their five hundredth.

THE POWER OF THE FETISH

THE ZUNI USE FETISHES for many purposes. Some enable hunters to catch game. Some make that game more plentiful. Fetishes can also play an integral part in curing ceremonies. They may protect not only an individual but the community as well. Abundance and fertility and, associatively, rain and bountiful crops are blessings a fetish can ensure.

Native Americans have always felt a special connection to nature. The belief that all things have a spirit is an integral part of their religions. The Zuni believe that animals are more like the Zuni deities than is man. They also believe that animals have more power than man and that these powers, both practical and spiritual, reside in their fetishes.

The protective or healing animals and the hunting or prey animals form two major groupings of fetishes. Protective and healing animals include the mountain lion, the bear, the badger, the wolf, the eagle, and the mole. All four directions plus the sky and underground have a protective animal associated with them. The north is protected by the mountain lion, the west by the bear, the south by the badger, the east by the wolf, the sky by the eagle, and the underground by the mole. Each direction also has its own specially related color. The north's color is yellow, the west is blue, the south is red, the east is white, the sky is all colors, and the underground is black. When an animal shares the same color as its primarily associated direction, that animal is considered the "elder brother" of all like animals. For example, the Yellow Mountain Lion is the elder brother of the Blue Mountain Lion. This continues counterclockwise around the compass points with the Blue Mountain Lion being the elder brother of the Red Mountain Lion and so on.

The hunting and prey animals include the mountain lion, the coyote, the bobcat, the wolf, the eagle, and the mole. Their hierarchy follows the protective and healing animals' pattern, except that the coyote replaces the bear as the west animal, and the bobcat replaces the badger as the south animal. The diagrams help to explain these relationships.

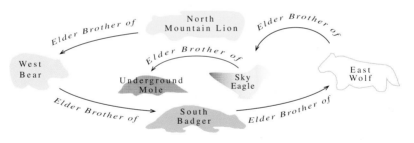

PROTECTIVE AND HEALING ANIMALS

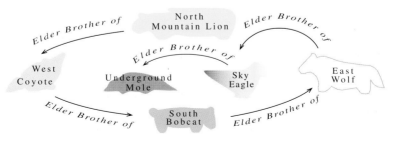

HUNTING ANIMALS

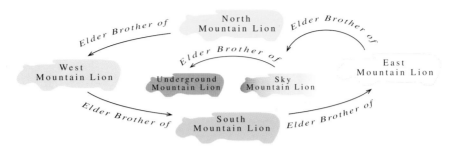

ELDER BROTHER RELATIONSHIPS
(EXAMPLE: MOUNTAIN LIONS)

Some animals are created with special features. An inlaid, carved, or painted "heartline" represents the breath path leading to the magical power in the fetish's heart. The hearts of hunting animals, for example, are believed to have magical power over the hearts of their prey, the game animals. The prey animals' breath (emanating from their hearts) is thought to overpower the game. A bundle consisting of various stones, shells, and/or arrowheads is sometimes tied onto a fetish. The bundle serves as an offering which empowers the fetish to better aid the user.

Personal fetishes were often worn or carried in pouches, but now they can also be found on mantles, in curio cabinets, and even in glove compartments. Fetishes usually had ceremonial feedings from the Zuni, the traditional food being corn pollen and crushed turquoise. Now regular food may provide this nourishment, with time and frequency varying from person to person.

The Zuni also have communal fetishes that are "owned" by different societies and clans. They are generally kept in "fetish pots" of a variety of shapes, including water storage jars (ollas, pronounced OY-yahs) or open bowl-shaped pieces. A hole cut into the side of the olla allows the fetishes inside to eat when food is presented to them outside of the jar.

I have heard of countless stories regarding the powers of fetishes, but some especially stand out in my mind. The mountain lion is believed to be the most powerful fetish a hunter can possess when stalking large game. I once met an Anglo man who related an interesting story about the first time he went hunting. Being inexperienced, he had gone to his Zuni friends for help. They gave him a mountain lion fetish and explained the rituals he must perform for it to work. The man followed their instructions for the preparatory ceremony before the hunt. He then drove to an open area and got out of his truck, gun in hand. At that moment, an antelope ran up, not ten feet away. Taking this as a sign, he shot and killed the animal and completed the rest of the ceremony. As soon as he had finished, two hunters ran up and exclaimed that they had been trailing that antelope for a long time. They wondered how he had been so lucky!

Bear fetishes perform some of the most important healing roles at Zuni. One woman I knew was diagnosed with terminal, inoperable cancer. She was told she had only a short time to live. Friends gave her a white bear, which the Zuni consider especially powerful. She kept it with her constantly in the hospital and after she was sent home to die. She lived four more years with that bear fetish at her side. I met another woman also diagnosed with cancer. She immediately purchased a turquoise bear fetish, since blue bears are the elder brother of all bears. She carried it with her to her next doctor's visit, and the cancer had disappeared.

The beliefs concerning owl fetishes differ by tribe, but the Zuni sometimes see them as home protectors. Several people I knew from the Los Angeles area purchased owl fetishes, independently. Shortly after the disastrous earthquake of January 1994 each customer returned and described how their house had remained intact or received little damage. They all said their neighbors' homes, however, had been seriously damaged.

While there are many interesting stories about fetishes, unfortunately over the last few years misinformation has circulated about their functions. This includes non-Zuni concepts attributed to Zuni fetishes. It is inaccurate to attribute powers and psychological properties of Euro-American origin to a Zuni fetish and claim that the Zuni believe the same. Also, interpreting what other tribes believe about an animal and assuming that the Zuni agree would be like assuming that Jews and Christians share the same beliefs about pigs.

A fetish can represent anything you, as the possessor, want it to represent. It can also have whatever "powers" you so desire. Your strength of belief will likely constitute the most important factor in the efficacy of the fetish. But power is only one of the reasons people buy fetishes. They are most commonly purchased as charming works of art.

MOUNTAIN LIONS

Peter and Dinah Gasper,
alabaster

Protective and Hunting Animal of the North

MOUNTAIN LION FETISHES vary the most in usage of all the animal fetishes. They are essential to hunters in the taking of big game, especially deer, elk, buffalo, and mountain sheep. Zuni warriors carried them, and they are believed to protect travelers on their journeys (sort of the Zuni St. Christopher). The mountain lion is considered the elder brother of all the other protective and hunting animals. Originally mountain lions were carved with their tails forming a central ridge up their backs. Now they are also carved with tails slung over the back and down the side or hanging down from the back. Their tails are narrow, not thick or bushy.

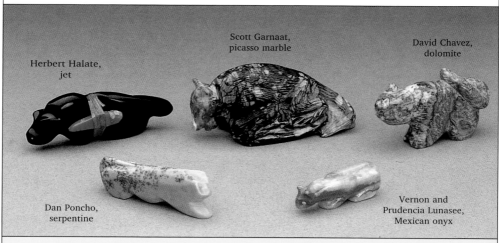

Scott Garnaat,
picasso marble

David Chavez,
dolomite

Herbert Halate,
jet

Dan Poncho,
serpentine

Vernon and
Prudencia Lunasee,
Mexican onyx

MOUNTAIN LION ELDER BROTHER IS YELLOW

Brian Ahiyite,
black marble

PROTECTIVE ANIMAL OF THE WEST

BEAR FETISHES are one of the most important fetish animals throughout the Southwest. They probably comprise the most commonly carved fetish subject because so many Native and non-Native Americans feel an affinity for them. Initiates of the Bear Clan (or Bear Society) in many Pueblo cultures become members of what might be called the equivalent of the American Medical Association. While all bears have great curative abilities, white bears provide especially powerful healing. Generally bear fetishes will have little or no tails but quite a range of body shapes.

BEAR ELDER BROTHER IS BLUE

Randy Lucio,
picasso marble

Vince Chavez,
alabaster

Alvin Haloo,
picasso marble

Ernest Peina,
picasso marble

Florentino Martinez
and Harrietta Byers,
pipestone

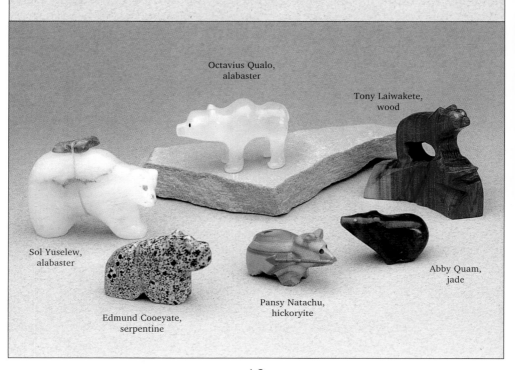

Octavius Qualo,
alabaster

Tony Laiwakete,
wood

Sol Yuselew,
alabaster

Abby Quam,
jade

Edmund Cooeyate,
serpentine

Pansy Natachu,
hickoryite

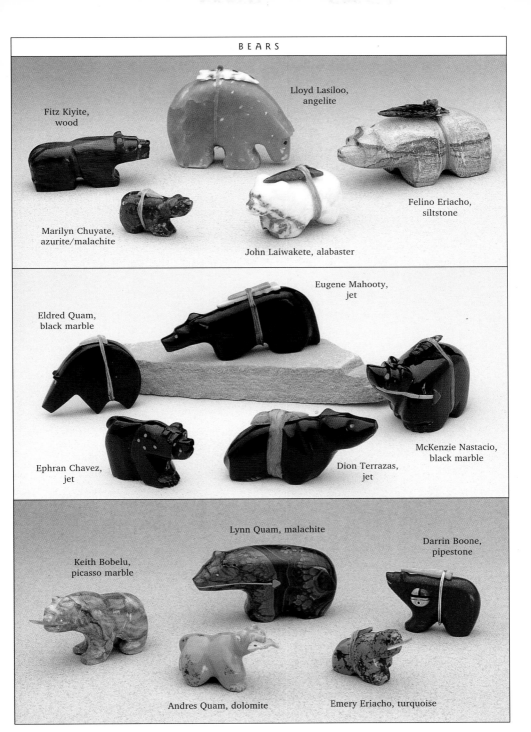

BEARS

Fitz Kiyite,
wood

Lloyd Lasiloo,
angelite

Marilyn Chuyate,
azurite/malachite

John Laiwakete, alabaster

Felino Eriacho,
siltstone

Eldred Quam,
black marble

Eugene Mahooty,
jet

Ephran Chavez,
jet

Dion Terrazas,
jet

McKenzie Nastacio,
black marble

Keith Bobelu,
picasso marble

Lynn Quam, malachite

Darrin Boone,
pipestone

Andres Quam, dolomite

Emery Eriacho, turquoise

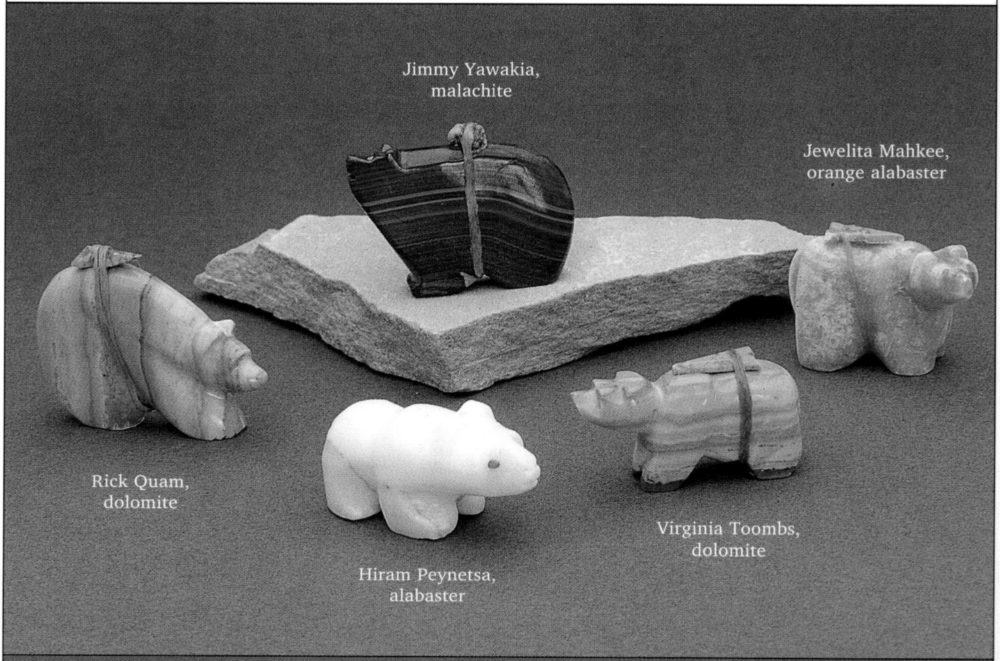

Jimmy Yawakia,
malachite

Jewelita Mahkee,
orange alabaster

Rick Quam,
dolomite

Virginia Toombs,
dolomite

Hiram Peynetsa,
alabaster

Colvin Peina,
picasso marble

Rickson
Kalestewa,
alabaster

Leonard Halate,
jasper

Melissa Quam,
dolomite

Loubert Soseeah and Rosella Lunasee,
red "serpentine marble"

BADGERS

PROTECTIVE ANIMAL OF THE SOUTH

BADGER FETISHES are not as common in Pueblo cultures as those of the mountain lion and bear. It is believed that the badger helps medicine men and shamans dig the roots and herbs needed in healing. Their fetishes are usually carved fairly low to the ground with somewhat bushy tails and pointed noses. I have heard their carvings likened to "flat wolves." Badger fetishes at one time were hard to find but now are appearing with greater frequency.

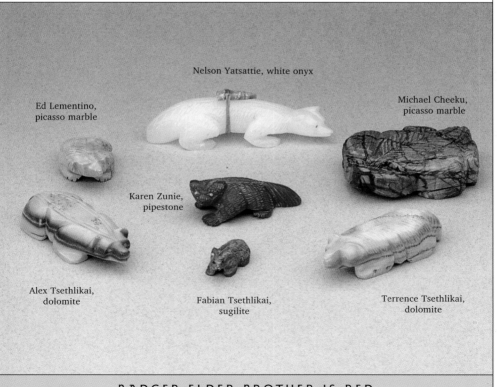

Nelson Yatsattie, white onyx

Ed Lementino, picasso marble

Michael Cheeku, picasso marble

Karen Zunie, pipestone

Alex Tsethlikai, dolomite

Fabian Tsethlikai, sugilite

Terrence Tsethlikai, dolomite

BADGER ELDER BROTHER IS RED

WOLVES

David Tsikewa,
Zuni stone
(travertine)

PROTECTIVE AND HUNTING ANIMAL OF THE EAST

WOLF FETISHES are used by many Pueblo tribes. They have very strong hunting powers and may be carried by Zuni hunters when antelope or some larger game are the prey. The carvings generally feature longish, hanging tails which are thick and full, but some carvers give their wolves upturned tails. Older wolf fetishes often had shorter thinner tails, and a few artists continue to use this style today. In other words, there is a great variety in their appearance, so they are not always easily recognized by collectors.

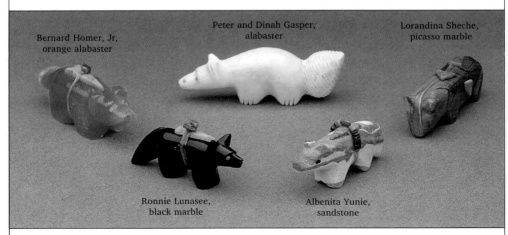

Bernard Homer, Jr,
orange alabaster

Peter and Dinah Gasper,
alabaster

Lorandina Sheche,
picasso marble

Ronnie Lunasee,
black marble

Albenita Yunie,
sandstone

WOLF ELDER BROTHER IS WHITE

16

EAGLES

PROTECTIVE AND HUNTING ANIMAL OF THE SKY

EAGLE FETISHES exist in a number of Pueblo cultures. Hunters sometimes carry them for success when rabbits or other small game are their prey. Eagles may be called upon to carry a shaman in flight when his spirit leaves his body to search for the cause of a patient's illness. As carving tools have improved over the years, eagle fetishes have also changed in form. They were originally carved very simply and compactly, often with an "x" on their backs to symbolize their crossed wings. Now artists can create realistic eagles with upturned, out-stretched, or lowered wings reaching away from the body and with great detailing in the feathers.

Elfina Hustito,
picasso marble

Stewart Quandelacy,
dolomite

Aaron and Thelma Sheche,
dolomite

Lena Boone,
fluorite

Vernon and Prudencia Lunasee,
serpentine

EAGLE ELDER BROTHER IS ALL COLORS TOGETHER

PROTECTIVE AND HUNTING ANIMAL
OF THE UNDERGROUND

MOLE FETISHES seem uncommon among the Pueblo tribes. The mole (or shrew, which may be a more likely interpretation) helps protect growing crops by hunting mice, rodents, and other small game that damage those crops. The mole has the least power of all the protective and hunting animals. Moles are generally carved low to the ground, often with pointed noses. They can have fairly thin, pointed, or stubby tails. Although mole fetishes were rarely carved in years past, they appear more frequently now due to the increased demand from collectors looking to complete directional sets.

Aaron and Thelma Sheche,
picasso marble

Fred Weekoty,
picasso marble

Abby Quam,
black marble

Arvella Cheama,
picasso marble

Georgia Quandelacy,
amber

COYOTES

Hunting Animal of the West

WHILE THE COYOTE is known as a trickster in many Native American cultures, this has little to do with coyote fetishes and how they are used. Coyote fetishes can rarely be found at most Pueblos, but at Zuni they may be used when hunting rabbit. One story has it that mountain sheep were coyote's designated prey. When coyote failed to catch a mountain sheep set free especially for him, he was forced to give up his claim to the mountain lion who then caught the mountain sheep instead. Coyote was relegated to scavenging. Coyote fetishes originally were formed with longish, straight-back tails but now are usually carved in a howling position.

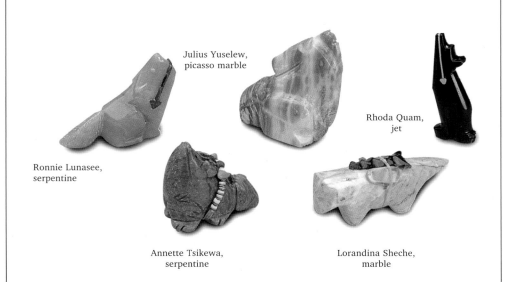

Julius Yuselew,
picasso marble

Rhoda Quam,
jet

Ronnie Lunasee,
serpentine

Annette Tsikewa,
serpentine

Lorandina Sheche,
marble

COYOTE ELDER BROTHER IS BLUE

BOBCATS

Hunting Animal of the South

THE BOBCAT (or wildcat or even lynx, depending on different viewpoints) is another uncommon animal fetish among the Pueblo peoples. For some reason the bobcat is, and always has been, one of the rarest of the fetish animals. At Zuni, the bobcat can be used when antelope is the prey. Bobcats originally were carved with shortish, straight-back tails and flat faces. Now they are often crafted in great detail, usually with whiskers protruding from either side of the face and a bobbed tail.

Michael Coble,
picasso marble

Wilfred Cheama,
serpentine

Dan Quam,
picasso marble

Lorandina Sheche, picasso marble

Dan Poncho, serpentine

BOBCAT ELDER BROTHER IS RED

FROGS AND TURTLES

BOTH FROG AND TURTLE CARVINGS appeared in pre-historic times as jewelry. The Hohokam were prolific producers of shell frogs, carving the shell so that the domed half became the body of the frog. Considered one of, if not the major rain-bringing fetish, the frog is also associated with abundance and fertility. While fertility is not its main function, I have heard of women who became pregnant while purposely keeping a frog fetish by their bed. Turtles also have a rain association in addition to serving as a link to the Zuni ancestors. Frog and turtle fetishes are some of the most frequently carved at Zuni.

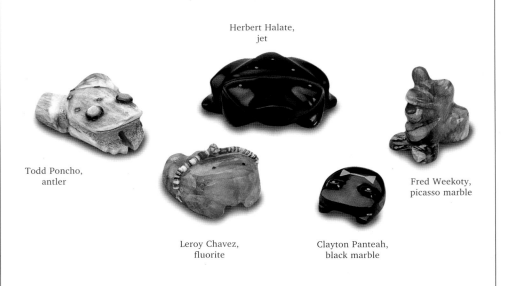

Herbert Halate,
jet

Todd Poncho,
antler

Leroy Chavez,
fluorite

Clayton Panteah,
black marble

Fred Weekoty,
picasso marble

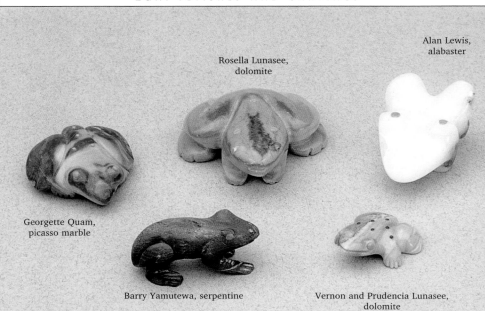

Rosella Lunasee,
dolomite

Alan Lewis,
alabaster

Georgette Quam,
picasso marble

Barry Yamutewa, serpentine

Vernon and Prudencia Lunasee,
dolomite

Karen Hustito,
picasso marble

Cato Pinto,
serpentine

Faylena Cachini,
alabaster

Daisy Natewa,
alabaster

Joel Nastacio,
alabaster

Max Laate,
antler

Russell Shack,
pipestone

Rhoda Quam,
turquoise

Christine Banteah,
picasso marble

Loren Burns,
mother-of-pearl
and turquoise

Marilyn Chuyate,
serpentine

Darren Shebola,
pipestone

Reynold Lunasee,
dolomite

Angel Yatsayte,
serpentine

Lebert Kaskalla,
picasso marble

Al Lasiloo,
serpentine

SNAKES

Alex Poncho,
black marble

SNAKE FETISHES have widespread usage throughout the Southwestern Pueblo cultures, possessing curative powers in some tribes. At Zuni, snakes are associated with the lightning that usually accompanies our dramatic Southwestern thunderstorms. Snake fetishes can be coiled, slightly curving, or slithering. Many are done in great detail now, unlike the simple shapes of old serpent fetishes which were often formed from the curved parts of deer antlers. The old fetishes were more likely the rain-associated Plumed or Water Serpent rather than the rattlesnake we usually see carved today.

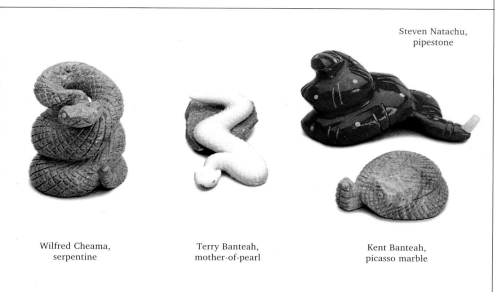

Steven Natachu,
pipestone

Wilfred Cheama,
serpentine

Terry Banteah,
mother-of-pearl

Kent Banteah,
picasso marble

OWLS AND OTHER BIRDS

To Native Americans, owls are somewhat like anchovies. You either love them or you hate them. Some Native American groups perceive owls as harbingers of death, while others may see them as guardians of both the home and the village, hooting to warn villagers of approaching enemies. Many different types of bird fetishes appear at Zuni, including birds not intended to be any specific species. Hawks, falcons, and ground owls, while rarely carved, have hunting powers. Most birds are believed to carry prayers to the clouds and sky, asking for rain and blessings.

Christine Banteah,
picasso marble

Vivella Cheama,
picasso marble

Craig Haloo,
antler

Bernard Homer, Jr,
Zuni stone
(older style)

Willard Laate,
antler

Arvella Cheama,
picasso marble
hummingbird

Darrin Boone,
cowrie shell duck

Garrick Weeka,
antler turkey

Vivella Cheama,
picasso marble roadrunner

Calvert Bowannie
and Pedia Nastacio,
black marble raven

GAME ANIMALS

Max Laate,
antler antelope

BUFFALO, MOUNTAIN SHEEP, DEER, ANTELOPE, ELK, AND RABBITS

FETISHES OF THE GAME SPECIES help increase the numbers of each animal so the Zuni will have plenty to eat. The function of the hunting or prey animal fetishes is to help catch these animals. Deer, antelope, and elk were infrequently carved in the past, because the tools in use at the time did not allow sculpting fragile horns without breakage. Now that carving tools have improved, more of these fetishes can be carefully crafted in great detail.

Vernon and Prudencia
Lunasee, silverado
jet buffalo

Raybert Kanteena,
alabaster buffalo

Clive Hustito,
serpentine
buffalo

Rickson Kalestewa,
alabaster ram

Justin Red Elk,
jet ram

Pernell Laate,
antler
deer

Loubert Soseeah,
picasso marble ram

Elton Kaamasee,
antler elk

Gordon Poncho,
dolomite rabbit

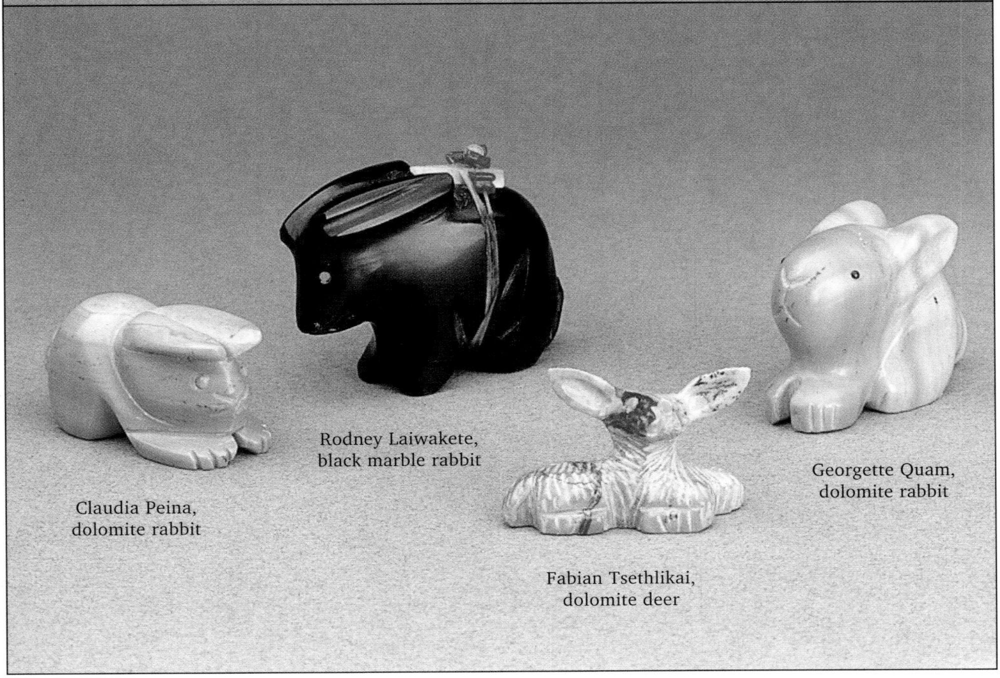

Ulysses Mahkee,
pipestone ram

Rodney Laiwakete,
black marble rabbit

Claudia Peina,
dolomite rabbit

Georgette Quam,
dolomite rabbit

Fabian Tsethlikai,
dolomite deer

DOMESTICATED ANIMALS

HORSES, SHEEP, GOATS, AND COWS

WHILE ALL OF THESE domesticated animal fetishes are carved at Zuni, their usage is most common among the Navajo (or Diné, pronounced deh-NEH). Several Zuni carvers over the years specialized in supplying a steady stream of these fetishes to traders who sold them to the Navajo. The Navajo still use them to protect their herds and flocks from disease, injury, and death or to help increase the numbers of their animals. Navajos will sometimes make these fetishes for themselves or even purchase store-bought replicas if necessary

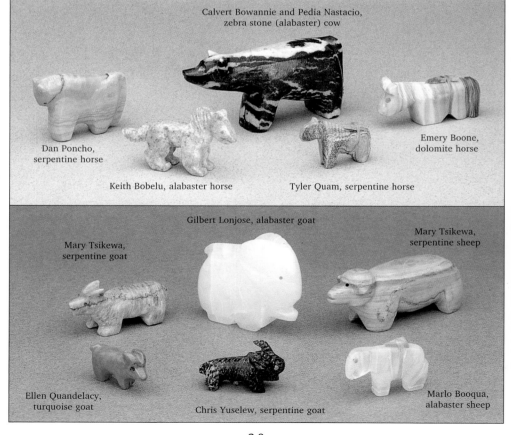

Calvert Bowannie and Pedia Nastacio,
zebra stone (alabaster) cow

Dan Poncho,
serpentine horse

Keith Bobelu, alabaster horse

Tyler Quam, serpentine horse

Emery Boone,
dolomite horse

Gilbert Lonjose, alabaster goat

Mary Tsikewa,
serpentine goat

Mary Tsikewa,
serpentine sheep

Ellen Quandelacy,
turquoise goat

Chris Yuselew, serpentine goat

Marlo Booqua,
alabaster sheep

LOCAL ANIMALS

THE ZUNI CREATE many different animal carvings today. Animals such as beaver, lizards, and horned toads, while often part of Zuni mythology, are not generally "fetish" animals in the same sense that the carvings mentioned earlier are. Their images are not usually kept to provide a specific benefit or blessing to the owner. Yet Zuni fetish carvers, like most other artists, often desire to try something different and challenging. Some of the finest contemporary carvings in this genre are of reptiles with almost life-like realism.

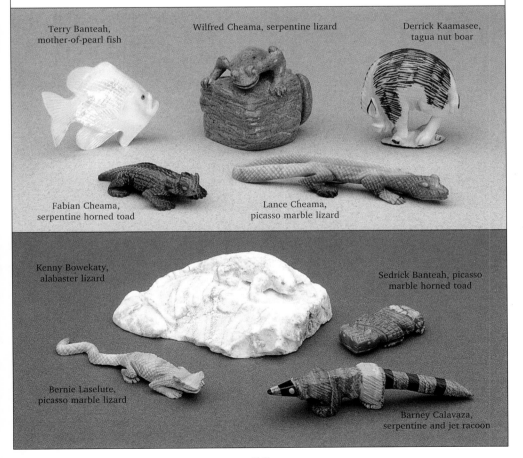

Terry Banteah, mother-of-pearl fish

Wilfred Cheama, serpentine lizard

Derrick Kaamasee, tagua nut boar

Fabian Cheama, serpentine horned toad

Lance Cheama, picasso marble lizard

Kenny Bowekaty, alabaster lizard

Sedrick Banteah, picasso marble horned toad

Bernie Laselute, picasso marble lizard

Barney Calavaza, serpentine and jet racoon

NON-LOCAL ANIMALS

THIS IS THE AREA in which Zuni creativity is most rapidly expanding. Photographs and drawings in books have inspired incredibly detailed animals from far outside the area of Zuni contact and even outside the realm of reality. From alligators to whales to jackalopes, innovation and imagination are generating new and different creations almost daily. While these carvings do not play a part in Zuni religious tradition (although non-local animal carvings go back at least as early as the 1930's), they certainly speak well of Zuni ingenuity, skill, and adaptability.

Michael Coble,
picasso marble alligator

Max Laate,
antler jackalope

Derrick Kaamasee,
serpentine whale

Tracey Zunie,
picasso marble seal

Kenny Chavez,
serpentine manta ray

Peter Natachu, Jr,
serpentine and pen shell
dinosaur

Derrick Kaamasee,
serpentine sea horse

Monica Soseeah,
black marble
dolphin

Lorie Bobelu,
picasso marble
shark

Eddington Hannaweeke,
turquoise hippopotamus

CORN MAIDENS AND MAIDENS

THE CORN MAIDENS are said to have secretly emerged with the Zuni from their previous existence in the Underworld. After a while, the Corn Maidens and the Zuni became separated, and witches destroyed the Zuni's crops. The twin sons of the Sun Father set out to find the maidens. After a long search they were found, and the Twins asked them to bring corn back to the Zuni people. So the Corn Maidens returned to save the Zuni from starvation. Other maidens carved represent Zuni and Hopi women. Both types of figures have recently gained popularity at Zuni, and some of the best artists produce quite graceful figurines.

Colvin Peina,
spiny oyster shell
maiden

Sandra Quandelacy,
turquoise
corn maiden
bundle

Todd Westika,
antler corn maiden
with tablita

Faye Quandelacy,
green seasnail shell
double-sided
corn maiden
and maiden

Levies Natewa,
picasso marble
corn maiden

THE ART OF CARVING

T HE ZUNI STYLE of fetish carving has changed considerably over the years. Originally fetishes had simple, abstract features. As fetishes were produced less for religious usage and more for sale to non-Native Americans, the public's desire for realism and "perfection" created a completely new look. In the 1930's, some carvers began to produce increasingly well-crafted pieces, the artist Leekya Deyuse (LEEK-yah DAY-you-see) among them. Fifty years later, carvers such as Dan Quam (KWAM) and the Cheama (chee-AH-ma) family started creating realistic animals. Other artists let their imaginations expand to make anything from sea creatures to dinosaurs. While some carvers produce more detailed renderings, others have done the opposite, reverting to the older and plainer style of fetishes.

Tools and methods involved in carving have improved greatly, making the carver's task easier. Modern cutting and polishing equipment has replaced the hand tools of the past. Today the stone is first sawed into a slab if the piece is large. If it is small, the material is trimmed down by saw. Some carvers draw an outline directly on the slab. Grinding off the stone to a rough-finished stage is next. Most artists now use a rubber-bond polishing wheel to smooth the piece and polish with a polishing compound on a buffing wheel. Any bundle attached to the fetish goes on last. The photograph to the right shows these stages in the creation of a "double coyote" fetish.

Another major evolution in carving has been the growing variety of materials available. Twenty-five years ago, Zuni artists worked in a limited range of serpentine, travertine, alabaster, jet, turquoise, azurite, coral, pipestone, antler, varieties of shell, and a few types of "found" stone. Today artists can choose among many unusual rocks and minerals from around the world. Sugilite, lapis lazuli, amber, angelite, charoite, opal, jade, rhodochrosite, and a wide array of marbles, dolomites, and onyxes have expanded the carving selection. In the past, materials were either found locally or supplied by a few regional traders. Now stone merchants frequently introduce new stones into the community.

The greatest difference in Zuni fetish carving today is probably the vast increase in the number of carvers. Twenty years ago there may have been about forty. That number is now about 300 full- and part-time carvers, and it grows every month. With this explosion in the number of artists has come a commensurate increase in the variety of styles. In the past, a trader or experienced collector could usually recognize almost every carver's work. It has become much more difficult to do that today.

Many carvers maintain a distinctive style that can be spotted easily. There are several diagnostic traits to look for in determining a fetish's creator. How is the head turned? What kind of expression does the face have? How pointed is the nose? How rounded or flat is the body? Is there a heartline? If a bundle is included, how is it constructed?

The popularity of fetishes has increased dramatically over the last fifteen years because of their spiritual and artistic appeal. A number of dedicated traders and retailers have helped bring about this public awareness. They saw the special quality in fetishes and encouraged their production and sale. This popularity has enabled an ever-increasing number of Zuni to make a living by carving. It has also allowed the collecting of fetishes as an art form to become much more accepted.

These double coyotes carved by Lorandina Sheche from picasso marble show the typical sequence of steps in the carving process. Many carvers carve without a drawn pattern.

1) Slab sawing for larger pieces or trim sawing for smaller pieces.

2) More trimming.

3) Grinding off the excess to the rough-finished stage.

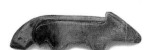

4) Smoothing with a rubber-bond polishing wheel.

5) Polishing with polishing compound.

6) Final polishing and attachment of offering.

THE TEDDY WEAHKEE FAMILY

Edna Leki,
septarian wolf

Teddy Weahkee,
Zuni stone eagle

Anderson Weahkee,
picasso marble
mountain lion

THE WEAHKEE (wee-AH-kee) family of carvers comprises one of the most important at Zuni. Not only does it consist of many talented artists, but marriage has linked it to many of the other early carving families. Teddy Weahkee, who died in 1965, was a major carver in the middle decades of this century. Primarily an independent craftsperson, he did not work for one specific trader for any length of time. He was known not only for his traditional fetishes, but for his inlaid jewelry, turquoise human figurines, carvings set into jewelry, and paintings.

Two of Teddy's daughters also became fetish carvers. One is Edna Leki (LEE-kee) whose family is best known for "old-style" carvings. They also do beautiful stringing fetishes for necklaces and some sleek, contemporary work as well. Edna's daughter Lena married Rignie Boone (now deceased) who was related to carvers Leekya Deyuse and Jimmy Boone.

Teddy's other daughter Mary Tsikewa (now deceased) was married to the late David Tsikewa (SIGH-kee-wah). They both produced work for traders Joe Tanner and the Kirk family. David was especially famous for his fetish necklaces. Members of this branch of the family create stringing fetishes as well as standing fetishes.

Teddy Weahkee's nephew Leo Poblano (pah-BLAH-no), who died in 1959 while fire-fighting, gained fame both as a fetish carver and as a maker of inlaid jewelry. He produced work for several traders including the Wallaces and the Woodards. Some of the finest and most intricate early inlay work done at Zuni was created by this talented artist. He carved in a wide variety of styles, so much so that his fetishes have become confused with and sold as those of other carvers of the time, such as his uncle Teddy Weahkee or Leekya Deyuse. Leo Poblano was married for a while to the late Daisy Hooee Nampeyo, a well-known Hopi potter. His last wife, Ida, worked on many of his later pieces with him.

The late Old Man Acque (AY-kew), another early fetish carver, was also related by marriage to the Weahkee family. While perhaps not as well known as some of his contemporaries, he produced a unique, traditional style. Unfortunately, some dealers have imitated his style and sell these copies as old fetishes. Members of the Acque family continue carving today.

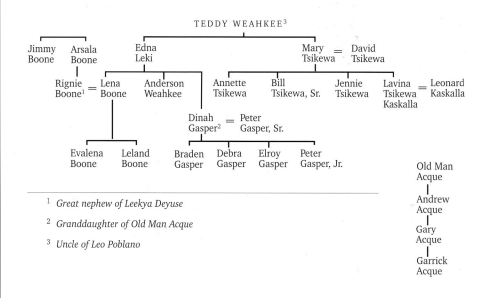

TEDDY WEAHKEE[3]

[1] *Great nephew of Leekya Deyuse*

[2] *Granddaughter of Old Man Acque*

[3] *Uncle of Leo Poblano*

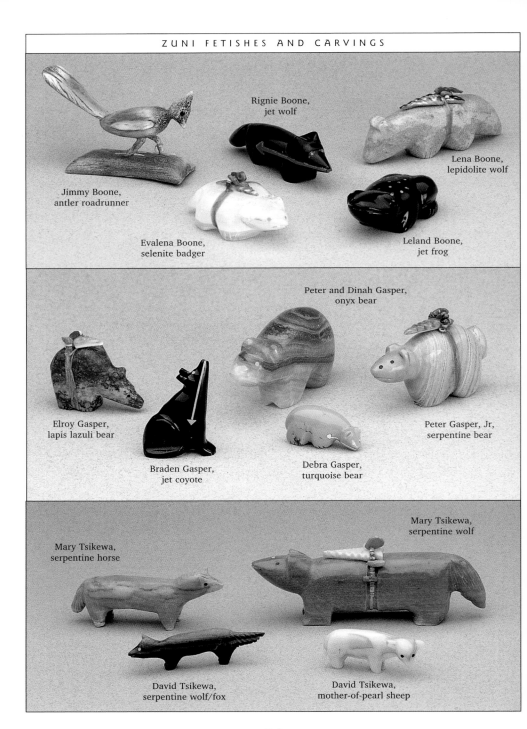

Jimmy Boone,
antler roadrunner

Rignie Boone,
jet wolf

Lena Boone,
lepidolite wolf

Evalena Boone,
selenite badger

Leland Boone,
jet frog

Elroy Gasper,
lapis lazuli bear

Braden Gasper,
jet coyote

Peter and Dinah Gasper,
onyx bear

Debra Gasper,
turquoise bear

Peter Gasper, Jr,
serpentine bear

Mary Tsikewa,
serpentine horse

Mary Tsikewa,
serpentine wolf

David Tsikewa,
serpentine wolf/fox

David Tsikewa,
mother-of-pearl sheep

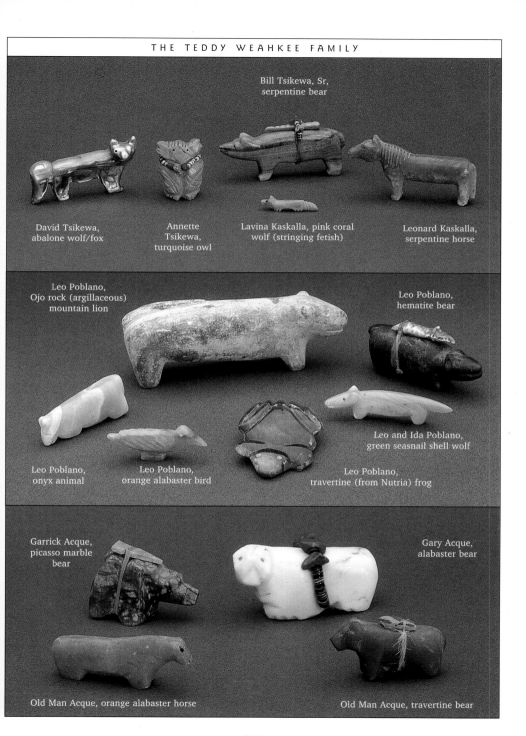

Bill Tsikewa, Sr,
serpentine bear

David Tsikewa,
abalone wolf/fox

Annette
Tsikewa,
turquoise owl

Lavina Kaskalla, pink coral
wolf (stringing fetish)

Leonard Kaskalla,
serpentine horse

Leo Poblano,
Ojo rock (argillaceous)
mountain lion

Leo Poblano,
hematite bear

Leo Poblano,
onyx animal

Leo Poblano,
orange alabaster bird

Leo and Ida Poblano,
green seasnail shell wolf

Leo Poblano,
travertine (from Nutria) frog

Garrick Acque,
picasso marble
bear

Gary Acque,
alabaster bear

Old Man Acque, orange alabaster horse

Old Man Acque, travertine bear

THE LEEKYA DEYUSE FAMILY

Leekya Deyuse,
travertine sheep

LEEKYA DEYUSE (LEEK-yah DAY-you-see) was probably the most famous fetish carver in the history of Zuni. He worked for many years for noted Zuni traders C. G. Wallace and the Kirk family, producing some of the finest carvings in Zuni up to that time. He also created beautiful fetish necklaces, turquoise figurines, and pieces set into jewelry, including leaves, animals, birds, and hands. His carvings became even more refined after he began using better equipment later in life. He died in 1966, but his artistry continues to be shown in countless books, magazines, and museums. His is the one name known by people not overly familiar with the genre. His work brings some of the highest prices on the "old" fetish market, even though it can only be recognized by style and not by signature. Because of the value and popularity of Leekya's work, fakes (usually poorly copied) are not uncommon. Carvings by members of his family are often sold, intentionally or unintentionally, as his. While certainly influenced by Leekya, their works are different creations and should be appreciated in their own right.

Leekya's daughter Sadie married Morris Laahty (lay-AH-tee), a talented inlay jeweler who on very rare occasions would show off his lapidary prowess by carving fetishes. Neither is still alive. Leekya's daughter Alice (also now deceased) married Bernard Homer, Sr. In the Homer family, Lambert, Sr. and Lambert, Jr. were excellent inlay artists but rarely carved fetishes.

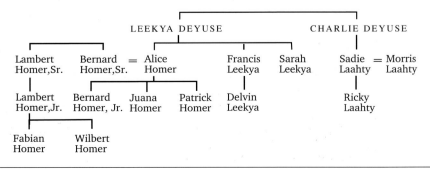

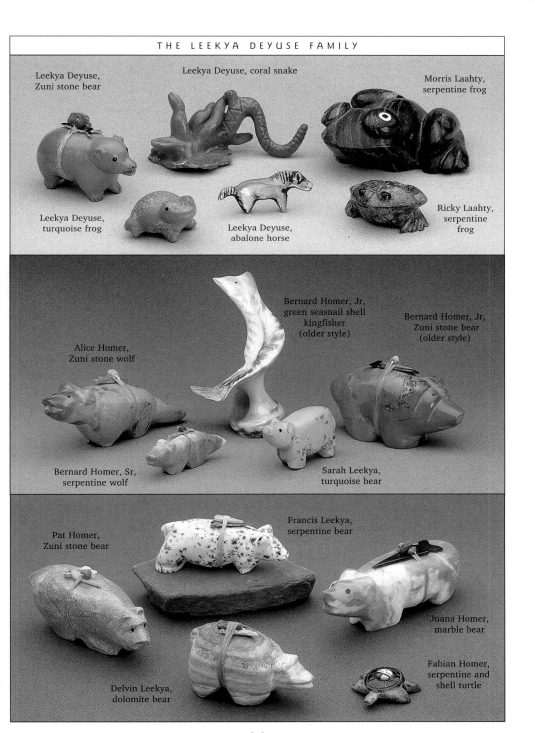

Leekya Deyuse,
Zuni stone bear

Leekya Deyuse, coral snake

Morris Laahty,
serpentine frog

Leekya Deyuse,
turquoise frog

Leekya Deyuse,
abalone horse

Ricky Laahty,
serpentine
frog

Alice Homer,
Zuni stone wolf

Bernard Homer, Jr,
green seasnail shell
kingfisher
(older style)

Bernard Homer, Jr,
Zuni stone bear
(older style)

Bernard Homer, Sr,
serpentine wolf

Sarah Leekya,
turquoise bear

Pat Homer,
Zuni stone bear

Francis Leekya,
serpentine bear

Juana Homer,
marble bear

Delvin Leekya,
dolomite bear

Fabian Homer,
serpentine and
shell turtle

39

THE THEODORE KUCATE FAMILY

Theodore Kucate,
travertine bobcat

THEODORE KUCATE (COO-kah-tee) was a recognized early carver at Zuni but was probably best known for the family dance troupe, which did traditional dances. His carvings, while very traditional, had a charming friendliness to them. Theodore's family continues to be very active in fetish carving, basing most of their work on Cushing's *Zuni Fetiches*. Both Theodore's and his son-in-law Aaron Sheche's (SHEE-shee) older style of carving is often copied by unscrupulous dealers and sold as old fetishes. These fakes are rarely attributed to any specific carver. Today the family's style is very homogeneous. It seems difficult to tell one family member's carving from another's unless initials are on the bottom of the piece. All of their work is pleasing.

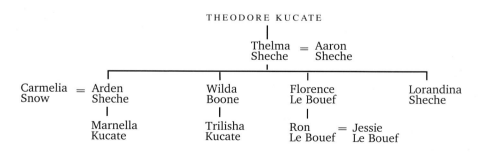

THEODORE KUCATE

Thelma = Aaron
Sheche   Sheche

Carmelia = Arden   Wilda   Florence   Lorandina
Snow   Sheche   Boone   Le Bouef   Sheche

           Marnella   Trilisha   Ron   = Jessie
           Kucate   Kucate   Le Bouef   Le Bouef

Theodore Kucate,
sandstone mountain lion

Theodore Kucate,
Ojo rock horse

Aaron Sheche,
travertine bear
(older style)

Theodore Kucate,
alabaster bear

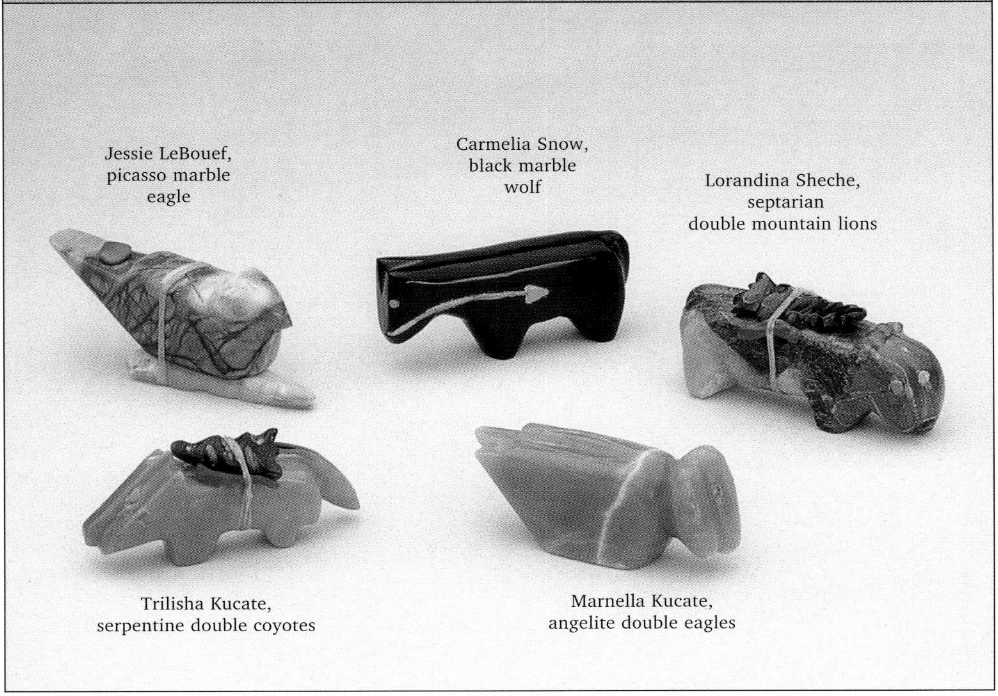

Aaron and Thelma Sheche,
serpentine double coyotes

Jessie LeBouef,
picasso marble
eagle

Carmelia Snow,
black marble
wolf

Lorandina Sheche,
septarian
double mountain lions

Trilisha Kucate,
serpentine double coyotes

Marnella Kucate,
angelite double eagles

THE QUANDELACY FAMILY

Andres Quandelacy,
amber wolf

THE QUANDELACY (KWAN-deh-LAY-see) family creates some of the most elegant fetishes in Zuni. Ellen Quandelacy learned the art of carving from her father, Johnny Quam, while her sister Annie Gasper Quam is a well-known jeweler. The children of both women took up fetish carving with a passion and produce a wide range of work from traditional to modern stylings. Stewart Quandelacy's bears have almost become the quintessential Zuni fetish. This family's artistry has helped set the standard for much of contemporary fetish carving.

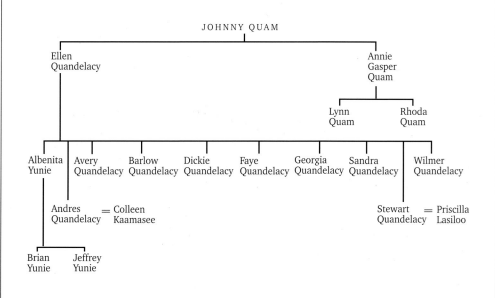

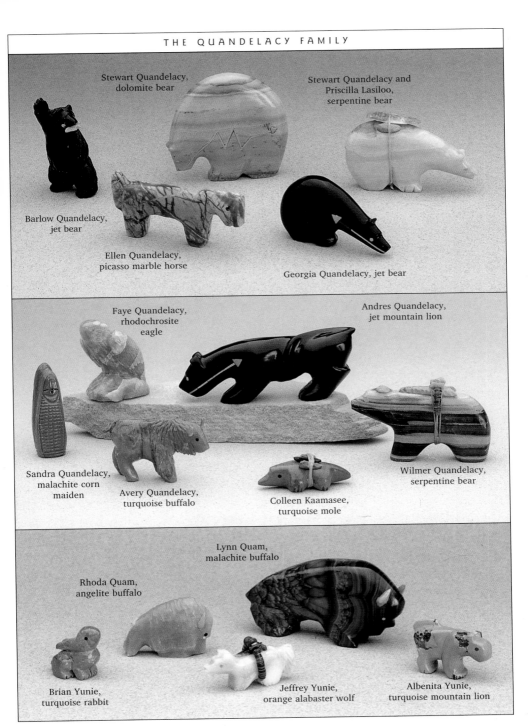

Stewart Quandelacy,
dolomite bear

Stewart Quandelacy and
Priscilla Lasiloo,
serpentine bear

Barlow Quandelacy,
jet bear

Ellen Quandelacy,
picasso marble horse

Georgia Quandelacy, jet bear

Faye Quandelacy,
rhodochrosite
eagle

Andres Quandelacy,
jet mountain lion

Sandra Quandelacy,
malachite corn
maiden

Avery Quandelacy,
turquoise buffalo

Colleen Kaamasee,
turquoise mole

Wilmer Quandelacy,
serpentine bear

Lynn Quam,
malachite buffalo

Rhoda Quam,
angelite buffalo

Brian Yunie,
turquoise rabbit

Jeffrey Yunie,
orange alabaster wolf

Albenita Yunie,
turquoise mountain lion

43

Many people think they will collect one or two fetishes, but this usually does not last for long. A directional set is often the next group of items purchased. People usually wind up with a range of animals, often owning multiples of their favorites. Some collectors specialize in certain animals. Collections of carving families is another popular method. A few people only purchase "old" fetishes, whether that means 10 or 100 years old. Some believe that these are "true" fetishes. However, fetishes began to be carved for sale to non-Native Americans not long after the railroad arrived. Exclusively "old" fetish collectors are also missing out on the exciting work of gifted contemporary artists.

Today a fetish collector can purchase almost any style, material, type of animal, or price range desired. An unfortunate consequence of the heightened interest in fetishes has been a rise in the number of imitation carvings from overseas, often sold as Native American handmade. The copies are usually very sharp-edged, a result of being sawbladed out quickly for cheap mass production. They are also frequently made of a so-called "block" material, which is nothing more than colored plastic cut into blocks for easy slabbing and shaping. Block plastic is patterned to look like turquoise, coral, jet, malachite, azurite, lapis lazuli, and spiny oyster shell, among others. Sadly, some Zuni carvers will also try to pass off block as the real thing.

Copying of Zuni fetishes by the Navajo has become an issue as well. While this has gone on for over twenty years, Navajo fetishes are sometimes misrepresented as Zuni, often through ignorance. The Navajo traditionally carved horse, sheep, and goat fetishes to protect their own herds and flocks. Many Navajo have purchased Zuni carvings of these animals for the same purpose. Larger wooden snake, human, and bird carvings were sometimes made for religious usage. I have seen bear fetishes with other Navajo religious articles, but so far, all the older ones were non-Navajo in origin. Many Navajo fetishes (other than those mentioned) may be seen as an attempt to capitalize on the commercial success of Zuni fetishes. Attributing Zuni meanings or directional and color associations to Navajo fetishes, although common, is inaccurate. The Navajo and the Zuni have different belief systems, and associating one with the other is a disservice to both. The buyer should be aware, however, that the Navajo have been strongly encouraged by Anglo traders to produce fetishes. And some do work in shops using mass production techniques.

After the initial stage of collecting, cataloging or note-taking becomes important. You may think that you will surely remember what the seller said about your fetish. But in a few days, that memory may fade unless the specifics were jotted down. Keep all your information together and accessible. Unfortunately, many stores do not know who carved the fetish or even what tribe the carving comes from. So be careful. The store should be able to tell you who carved it, what tribe the artist is from, what it is made of (and guarantee that the material is real), and what the fetish represents. It is also helpful to get information on the craftsperson and their family. Sometimes retailers make mistakes and inadvertently mislabel or misidentify a piece. If this is a consistent pattern, however, find another source for your purchases. Merchants who are truly interested in fetishes strive to keep current on new carvers and materials. They carefully purchase their fetishes from honest and accurate sources. And they are excited about fetishes and treat them as something special rather than just another commodity.

I have a simple rule of fetish selection: if the fetish "talks" to me, I buy it—no matter what the animal is or which Zuni carver made it. People have the mistaken idea that they pick out fetishes. I believe that fetishes usually pick you out. I have seen countless incidents where people have walked past a case of fetishes, suddenly pulled one out, and said, "I guess this one's supposed to be mine!" This usually happens to people who had no intention of buying.

One final thing to remember: simply because a carver's work does not appear in this or any other fetish book does not mean he or she is not a good carver. There probably wasn't an example of that person's work available at the time the carvings were photographed. A good artist evolves a unique way of giving character to a piece. But most importantly, a carver's work is "good" if it appeals to you.

BIBLIOGRAPHY

Bunzel, Ruth

    1932   *Introduction to Zuni Ceremonialism.* Washington, D.C.: Smithsonian Institution, Bureau of American Ethnology, 47th Annual Report 1929-30.

Cushing, Franklin Hamilton

    1883   *Zuni Fetiches.* Washington, D.C.: Smithsonian Institution, Bureau of American Ethnology, 2nd Annual Report 1880-81.

    1979   *Zuni: Selected Writings of Franklin Hamilton Cushing.* Edited by Jesse Green. Lincoln, NE: University of Nebraska Press.

Eggan, Fred and T. N. Pandy

    1979   "Zuni History, 1850-1970" in *Handbook of North American Indians, Vol. 9.* Edited by Alfonso Ortiz. Washington, D.C.: Smithsonian Institution.

Ellis, Florence Hawley

    1969   *Differential Pueblo Specialization in Fetiches and Shrines.* Mexico, D.F.: Anales del Instituto Nacional de Antropología e Historia, 1967-68, Sobretiro Septima Epoca Tomo 1.

Frisbie, Charlotte J.

    1987   *Navajo Medicine Bundles or Jish: Acquisition, Transmission and Disposition in the Past and Present.* Albuquerque, NM: University of New Mexico Press.

Kirk, Ruth F.

    1943   *Introduction to Zuni Fetishism.* Santa Fe, NM: Archaeological Institute of America, Papers of the School of American Research.

Kluckhorn, Clyde, W. W. Hill, and Lucy Wales Kluckhorn

    1971   *Navaho Material Culture.* Cambridge, MA: Belknap Press of the Harvard University Press.

Parsons, Elsie Clews

    1939   *Pueblo Indian Religion.* Chicago: University of Chicago Press.

    1964   *The Social Organization of the Tewa of New Mexico.* New York: American Anthropological Association, Krause Reprint Corp.

Rodee, Marian and James Ostler

    1990   *The Fetish Carvers of Zuni.* Albuquerque, NM: The Maxwell Museum of Anthropology, University of New Mexico.

Slaney, Deborah

    1993   "Zuni Figurative Carving from the C. G. Wallace Collection," Scottsdale, AZ: *American Indian Art Magazine,* Vol. 19, #1.

BIBLIOGRAPHY

Stevenson, Matilda Coxe

1904 *The Zuni Indians.* Washington, D.C.: Smithsonian Institution, Bureau of American Ethnology, 23rd Annual Report 1901-02.

Woodbury, Richard B.

1979 "Zuni Prehistory and History to 1850" in *Handbook of North American Indians Vol. 9.* Edited by Alfonso Ortiz. Washington, D.C.: Smithsonian Institution.

INDEX

Levies Natewa 31
Clayton Panteah 21
Claudia Peina 27
Colvin Peina 14, 31
Ernest Peina 12
Hiram Peynetsa 14
Cato Pinto 22
Ida Poblano 37
Leo Poblano 37
Alex Poncho 24
Dan Poncho 10, 20, 28
Gordon Poncho 27
Todd Poncho 21
Octavius Qualo 12
Abby Quam 12, 18
Andres Quam 13
Dan Quam 20
Eldred Quam 13
Georgette Quam 22, 27
Lynn Quam 13, 43
Melissa Quam 14
Rhoda Quam 19, 23, 43
Rick Quam 14
Tyler Quam 28
Andres Quandelacy 42, 43
Avery Quandelacy 43
Barlow Quandelacy 43
Ellen Quandelacy 28, 43
Faye Quandelacy 31, 43
Georgia Quandelacy 18, 43
Sandra Quandelacy 31, 43
Stewart Quandelacy 17, 43, front cover
Wilmer Quandelacy 43
Justin Red Elk 26
Russell Shack 23
Darren Shebola 23
Aaron Sheche 17, 18, 41
Lorandina Sheche 16, 19, 20, 33, 41
Thelma Sheche 17, 18, 41
Carmelia Snow 41

Loubert Soseeah 14, 27
Monica Soseeah 30
Dion Terrazas 13
Virginia Toombs 14
Alex Tsethlikai 15
Fabian Tsethlikai 15, 27
Terrence Tsethlikai 15
Annette Tsikewa 19, 37
Bill Tsikewa, Sr 37
David Tsikewa 16, 36, 37
Mary Tsikewa 28, 36
Anderson Weahkee 34
Teddy Weahkee 34
Garrick Weeka 25
Fred Weekoty 18, 21
Todd Westika 31
Barry Yamutewa 22
Nelson Yatsattie 15
Angel Yatsayte 23
Jimmy Yawakia 14
Albenita Yunie 16, 43
Brian Yunie 43
Jeffrey Yunie 43
Chris Yuselew 28
Julius Yuselew 19
Sol Yuselew 12
Karen Zunie 15
Tracey Zunie 30

_____

Lenny Chuyate
Lucy Cooeyate
Larry Delena
Lita Delena
Sam Delena
Sammie Delena
Howard Dutukewa
Brummett Epaloose
Faye Eriacho
Jeff Eriacho
Carl Etsate
Todd Etsate
Albert Eustace
Reva Halate
Vella Halate
Miguel Haloo
Ramie Haloo
Wayne Haloo
Herbert Him, Jr
Wilbert Homer
Alonzo Hustito
Herbert Hustito
Jack Kalestewa
Rose Kaamasee
Rosita Kaamasee
Libert Kaskalla
Dawn Laate
Jerrold Lahaleon
Donovan Laiwakete
Fernando Laiwakete
Averill Lamy
Alan Lasiloo
Mike Lasiloo
Mike Leekela
Loren Leekela
Joe Leekity
Tricia Leekity
Tim Lementino
Richard Leonard
Terry Leonard
Howard Lesarlley
Lorae Lonasee
Florenda Lonasee
Danny Lonjose
Gale Lucio
Jed Lucio
Ernie "Woody" Mackel
Tony Mackel
Lewis Malie
Drucilla Martinez
Victor Martza

Anthony Mecale
Esteban Najera
Joey Nastacio
Neil Natewa
Marjorie Nieto
Travis Nieto
Vern Nieto
Verna Noche
Tony Ohmsattie
Virginia Ohmsattie
Franklin Owelicio
Elroy Pablito
Kenny Panteah
Roxanne Panteah
Brandon Phillips
Marvellita Phillips
Herbert Pincion
Hubert Pincion
Veronica Poblano
Stephan Poncho
Andrew Quam
Andrew Emerson Quam
Dwight Quam
Gabriel Quam
Hubert Quam
Joey Quam
Johnny Quam
Laura Quam
Rosalia Quam
Sylvia Quam
Dickie Quandelacy
Arden Sheche
Jeff Shetima
Gabriel Sice
Augustine Terrazas
Raymond Tsethlikai
Vander Tsethlikai
Jennie Tsikewa
Terrence Tucson
Leroy Ukestine
Rose Vacit
Preston Walema
Louise Wallace
Pat Wallace
Emery Waseta
Darrell Westika
Myron Westika
Bernie Yamutewa
Brian Yatsattie
Mike Yatsayte
Rydell Yuselew